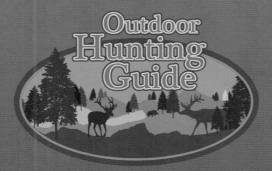

Outdoor Hunting Guide

Small Game

Janet Gurtler

MEDIA ENHANCED BOOKS
AV2 BY WEIGL™
ADDED VALUE • AUDIO VISUAL

www.av2books.com

MEDIA ENHANCED BOOKS
AV²
BY WEIGL™
ADDED VALUE • AUDIO VISUAL

AV² provides enriched content that supplements and complements this book. Weigl's AV² books strive to create inspired learning and engage young minds in a total learning experience.

Your AV² Media Enhanced books come alive with...

Audio
Listen to sections of the book read aloud.

Key Words
Study vocabulary, and complete a matching word activity.

Video
Watch informative video clips.

Quizzes
Test your knowledge.

Go to **www.av2books.com**, and enter this book's unique code.

BOOK CODE

H911203

Embedded Weblinks
Gain additional information for research.

Slide Show
View images and captions, and prepare a presentation.

AV² by Weigl brings you media enhanced books that support active learning.

Try This!
Complete activities and hands-on experiments.

... and much, much more!

Published by AV² by Weigl
350 5th Avenue, 59th Floor
New York, NY 10118
Website: www.weigl.com   www.av2books.com

Library of Congress Cataloging-in-Publication Data

Gurtler, Janet.
 Small game / Janet Gurtler.
    p. cm.
 Includes bibliographical references and index.
 ISBN 978-1-61913-504-8 (hard cover : alk. paper) — ISBN 978-1-61913-508-6 (soft cover : alk. paper) — ISBN 978-1-61913-699-1 (ebook)
 1. Small game hunting—Juvenile literature. I. Title.
 SK340.G87 2013
 799.2'5—dc23
                                  2012005576

Printed in the United States of America in North Mankato, Minnesota
1 2 3 4 5 6 7 8 9 16 15 14 13 12

062012
WEP170512

Project Coordinator: Aaron Carr
Art Director: Terry Paulhus

Every reasonable effort has been made to trace ownership and to obtain permission to reprint copyright material. The publishers would be pleased to have any errors or omissions brought to their attention so that they may be corrected in subsequent printings.

Weigl acknowledges Getty Images as its primary image supplier for this title.

Outdoor Hunting Guide

Small Game

Contents

What Is Small Game Hunting?

Hunting for small game means pursuing small animals for food or for sport. People may also hunt small game for their skins or furs. Sometimes, small game is trapped for **pest control**. In some cases, small game is hunted to make sure there are not too many animals living in one area.

Hunting is a tradition in some families. Older family members teach younger family members. Hunting small game, such as rabbits and squirrels, is how most beginners learn to hunt. Small-game hunting is an activity many people do with others. They enjoy being together outdoors with friends or family. Many hunters enjoy the exercise they get while tracking the animals. Hunting small game also gives people a chance to learn about nature.

Learning to hunt requires time and patience. Hunters learn about hunting rules and **conservation**. They figure out how the animals live and how to capture them. It takes practice to aim at and hit a target. Small-game hunters learn to use guns, bows and arrows, and even slingshots. Sometimes, hunters use traps.

Track the FACTS

The U.S. Fish and Wildlife Service reported that in 2006, there were more than 4.8 million hunters of small-game animals in the United States.

People in the United States spend more than $2 billion each year on small-game hunting trips and equipment.

Hunting seasons vary. In Kansas, cottontails can be hunted year-round, with a limit of 10 per day.

Focus on Small Game

Small game can include skunks, rabbits, woodchucks, squirrels, and some birds, such as grouse. Small-game animals are hunted for food and for their skins or **pelts**. Trappers capture furbearing animals, which include beavers, muskrat, mink, raccoons, coyotes, and red foxes.

The most hunted animal in North America is the cottontail rabbit. Rabbits are often found in open meadows near woods and in areas with small bushes and trees. There, they can hide from danger under the plants. Rabbits live in herds, and their homes are called warrens. Warrens are underground tunnels and rooms. Rabbits eat grasses, clover, berries, vegetables, tree buds, and bark.

Squirrels do not like open spaces. They prefer the woods, where they are protected. Squirrels build their nests in trees. They like areas with plants that have nuts and seeds. Squirrels also eat green shoots, mushrooms, fruits, and bark.

Raccoons live in wooded areas with streams and ponds nearby. They are omnivores, which means they eat both plants and animals. Raccoons make their homes in hollow trees, in tree branches, inside rock dens, or in the ground. They tend to be more active at night than during the day.

A raccoon's diet includes plants, mice, worms, nuts, and fish.

Small Game Animals

Rabbit

The eastern cottontail is the most common **species** of cottontail in North America. It is mainly found east of the Rocky Mountains.

Squirrel

Red squirrels live all over North America. Black squirrels and eastern gray squirrels live in the eastern part of the continent.

Red Fox

Red foxes are found in most of Canada and the United States. Few foxes live in desert areas or along the West Coast, however.

Coyote

Coyotes are **scavengers** and hunters. They live in many types of **habitats**, including forests, mountains, deserts, prairies, and farmlands. Coyotes are found in most of North America.

Beaver

Beavers live in rivers, ponds, small lakes, streams, and marshes. They are found in most of North America but cannot survive in Canada's Far North or in the deserts of the U.S. Southwest.

American Indians often sewed small skins together.

History

In early times, humans needed to hunt to survive. It was the only way that people could get meat for food. Early people made their hunting tools from stones and branches. Later, people made better weapons, such as spears and bows and arrows. Guns replaced these early hunting tools. With each development, it became possible to collect more meat than before.

Early people hunted many animals. For example, Native Peoples in North America hunted coyotes. They used every piece of the coyote, including the **hide** and bones. Many craft and clothing items were made from coyote fur. Native Peoples used the coyote's tail for hats and its meat for food. Many Native Peoples' stories are about coyotes. For example, one tribe's legend tells how the coyote taught humans to hunt. The early people respected small-game animals as well as the larger, more dangerous animals that they hunted.

When people began to raise animals and to farm food crops, hunting became less necessary. Though they did not need to hunt as much, people still enjoyed hunting. Hunting for sport became popular. The term *game* started to be used for animals that were hunted. Hunters held contests to see how much game they could collect. At some hunting events, hunters showed off their shooting skills.

1. North America's open spaces attracted hunters in the 1800s. Visitors traveled westward to hunt game in the plains. American Indians often served as guides to hunting parties. The hunting groups included government officials and people who were exploring the area for business opportunities.

2. In every part of the world, hunting has been an important part of history. The ancient Egyptians were some of the first people to think of hunting as both a way to get food and a sport.

TIMELINE

200,000 years ago Early peoples hunted with stones and spears to stay alive. They used all parts of the animals.

83,000–75,000 years ago People began to farm and raise animals. They relied less on hunting animals for food.

about 3,000 years ago Parks for hunting were set up for kings in the Middle East.

about 1,000 years ago In Europe, the kings started to make rules about where hunting could take place.

250 years ago Guns started to become more popular with hunters. Archery, or using bows and arrows, became a sport for hunting.

Tracking

Hunters must often track the animal they are trying to catch. Tracking means pursuing and locating an animal. To track small game, hunters study the habits of the animals. They know the time of day the animals are active. They also listen for noises and scan the woods for animal movements. Looking from right to left helps a hunter see as much as possible.

Hunters search the ground for prints made by animal paws. They look for the number of toes and the spacing between the toes in the print. This information helps them figure out which animal made the prints. The ground may also reveal an animal's droppings. The droppings show what the animal has been eating. Hunters learn what the droppings of certain animals look like.

Hunters move carefully in forests so that their prey does not hear them. They look for overturned stones, a sign that an animal has been in the area. They know the smells that go along with animal habitats. Hunters learn these tracking skills over time.

A good pair of hunting binoculars helps the hunter spot small game.

Animal Tracks

Animal tracks are the imprints an animal leaves on the ground or in snow. An animal can be identified by its tracks. Tracks can also indicate the direction an animal is traveling. They even show whether the animal was walking or running. Sometimes, tracks are not very clear. In those cases, other clues, such as droppings, can help identify an animal.

Rabbit

Tracks

The cottontail's front tracks are a bit smaller and more rounded than the back tracks.

Squirrel

Tracks

Squirrel tracks have a V shape. The squirrel has four claws in front and five in back.

Coyote

Tracks

The tracks of a coyote are similar to those of a dog, but coyote tracks are more pointed.

Beaver

Tracks

Beavers drag wood to make to make their dams and dens. This can leave a worn path on the ground.

Equipment and Clothing

Small-game hunting can be done with guns. A rifle fires a single bullet and is best for long-range shooting. A shotgun can fire many **pellets**. It is used for short-range shooting. A pellet gun uses air to shoot a steel ball. Also called a BB gun, it is used for hunting squirrels and rabbits. Hunters can also use a bow and arrow or a **crossbow**. It takes strength to pull back the bow.

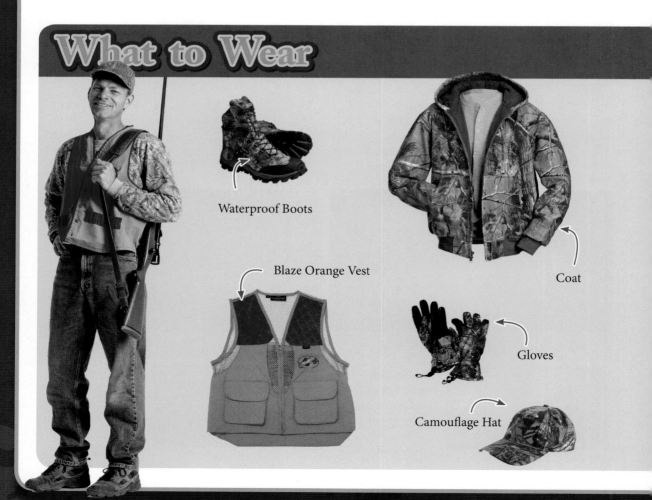

What to Wear

Waterproof Boots

Blaze Orange Vest

Coat

Gloves

Camouflage Hat

Hunting dogs can help the hunter. Labrador retrievers can find and bring back small game. Beagles can locate and chase rabbits. This is called beagling.

Hunters often wear camouflage clothing to stay hidden from the prey. These clothes are brown, green, or gray. They blend in with the surroundings. In some seasons, hunters must wear bright orange clothing. This color is called blaze orange. It helps hunters spot one another. In all seasons, layers of loose-fitting clothing help hunters stay comfortable in different conditions. In wet and cold weather, it is smart to keep head, neck, and shoulders covered. Waterproof boots and hats help keep hunters warm and dry.

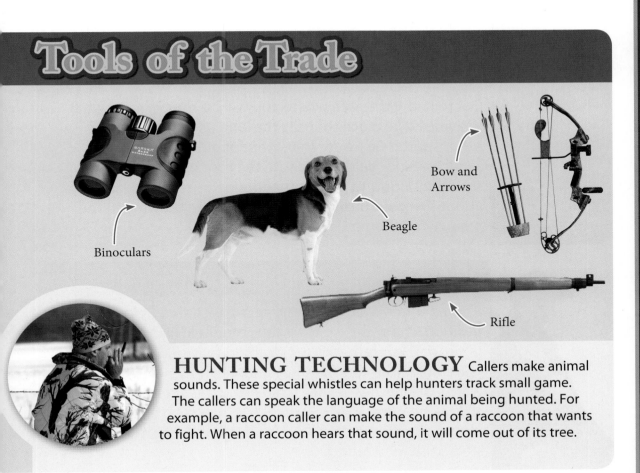

Tools of the Trade

Binoculars

Beagle

Bow and Arrows

Rifle

HUNTING TECHNOLOGY Callers make animal sounds. These special whistles can help hunters track small game. The callers can speak the language of the animal being hunted. For example, a raccoon caller can make the sound of a raccoon that wants to fight. When a raccoon hears that sound, it will come out of its tree.

Safety

Hunting safely is very important. No one should get hurt in the field or forest. Here are some basic safety tips.

Firearm Safety

Guns are dangerous weapons that should be handled with care. Learn as much as possible about the weapon that will be used before going hunting. Study how to hold the gun and control the trigger. Always act as if guns are loaded. Use a **trigger lock** when not firing. When not hunting, take the bullets out of the gun.

Safety in the Field and Forest

Get to know the area where you will be hunting and what activities take place there. Is the land used for hiking or other sports? Be aware that other people may be in the same forest or field. Make sure they are not nearby when shooting. Hunting holds other dangers, as well. Learn about the **poisonous** plants that may be growing in the area. Avoid them.

Weather Safety

A safe hunter is always aware of the weather. Before hunting, check the weather report on television, the radio, or the internet. Wear clothing that suits the weather conditions. The weather may change, however. Bring along warm, dry clothes in case it gets cold or starts to rain or snow. The hunting trip may take longer than expected. Take plenty of water to drink and food to eat. Bring matches to start a fire for warmth.

Safety in Numbers

It is always safer to hunt with others. In case of an accident, someone can help the injured person or go to get help. Hunters on their own should let someone know their plans. Someone should know where they are going and when they will return.

Be Sure of the Target

Hunters should always know what they are shooting at. They should never point a weapon at anything unless they are sure it is their prey. It is also important to be aware of what is beyond and around the prey. Do not fire at prey if another hunter is behind it. Hunters should wear something that is blaze orange. The bright color helps other hunters see them.

Track the FACTS

🐇 In Colorado, hunters must wear at least 500 square inches (3,230 square centimeters) of blaze orange clothing, and the items must include a hat.

🐇 There are more than 100 deaths from hunting accidents in North America each year.

🐇 In many areas, hunters can take safety courses to reduce the number of accidents. More than 30,000 people take hunting safety courses in Texas each year.

HUNTER CHECKLIST

1. hunting license
2. hunter education card
3. firearm or bow and arrows
4. bullets or pellets
5. binoculars
6. camouflage clothing
7. blaze orange clothing where required
8. gloves
9. Global Positioning System (GPS) device, map, and compass
10. knife
11. large plastic bag for game
12. food
13. water
14. flashlight and batteries
15. first aid kit
16. whistle
17. cell phone

A hunter must know as much as possible about any firearms in use.

Hunting Responsibly

All hunters must know and follow the rules for hunting small game. Government agencies regulate hunting. Before a hunting season begins, they set limits on the numbers that can be taken. There are different limits for each species. Officials want to make sure that each species continues to live. Different regions may have different rules. These rules may tell people where they are allowed to hunt. They may also say how many animals that a hunter may take at one time.

Many areas have rules against baiting animals. A hunter cannot put out food as bait to lure animals to one place. Luring the animals would make it easier to take them. Hunting responsibly includes following a code of fair chase. Fair chase means that the hunter does not have an unfair advantage. It means that the animal has a chance to get away.

Before shooting, it is important to know that the areas behind and around the target are clear.

When too many animals of one species are in an area, some animals may starve. In these cases, hunting can help with animal conservation. It controls the number of animals in an area. Varmint hunting is often done to control pests. Varmints are predators that take farm animals or damage crops. For example, foxes, prairie dogs, and groundhogs harm animals and crops. They may be hunted as varmints. In all cases, the hunter must take the animals as quickly as possible, so they do not suffer.

Small Game Careers

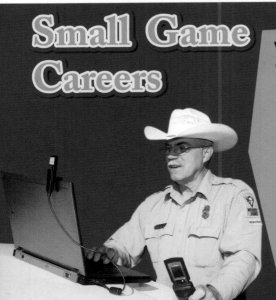

Wildlife Conservation Officer

Wildlife conservation officers are like the police of the forests. They make sure hunting laws are being followed. They also enforce laws that protect trees and prevent forest fires.

Wildlife conservationist officers usually have a college degree in science. Their studies focus on **biology** and **ecology**. They learn how humans and wildlife can live in harmony. Wildlife conservation officers should enjoy being in nature.

The Rules

Hunters are responsible for learning the rules of the area where they hunt. In many regions, hunters must pass a safety course and get a hunting license. The licenses state what rules must be followed. For example, it is often legal for people to hunt small game on their own farmlands. Hunting on someone else's land is illegal. Small-game licenses often allow hunters to take many types of animals. For example, coyotes, squirrels, rabbits, hares, opossums, weasels, skunks, and woodchucks may all be covered under one license.

New hunters must be led by experienced hunters.

Rules on how many animals can be caught in one day or in a season are called bag limits. Bag limits make sure that enough animals will live and have babies. This helps each species to survive. It also means that there will be enough animals for hunting in the future.

Always point the gun in a safe direction, so that no one will be hurt if it is fired by accident.

The hunting season for small game is often longer than for big game. One reason for the difference is that small game tends to live in larger numbers. Many types of small game give birth more often than large game do. Their numbers can be replaced more quickly.

Most hunting laws do not allow hunting before sunrise or after sunset. These rules may vary by area and the type of game being hunted. It can be hard to identify an animal in the dark. It is also more difficult to see whether other people are in an area.

Hunters who do not follow the rules and who take animals illegally are called poachers. Governments, conservation groups, and responsible hunters hope to stop poaching activities. Many officials urge people to report poachers.

Track the FACTS

🐇 In Manitoba, Canada, hunters do not need a license to hunt rabbits or gray squirrels. Hunting is also allowed on Sundays. In many other regions, the local rules do not allow hunting on Sundays.

🐇 Hunters can take any number of beavers throughout the year in Atlanta, Georgia.

🐇 In South Dakota, people can hunt coyotes throughout the year. They may even hunt them at night if they do not use electric lights.

After the Hunt

Small-game animals are often hunted for food. Several kinds of animals should be **dressed** soon after they are caught. Dressing keeps the meat from spoiling. A sharp knife helps the hunter skin and butcher the animal. Skinning and butchering animals can take practice. Hunters should always wear rubber gloves to keep their hands clean.

Some people want to keep the pelts of small animals. Different areas may have laws about this matter. Hunters must first check what the rules are before keeping and treating pelts.

Rabbit Stew

Ingredients
1 rabbit, about
   3 pounds (1.4 kilograms),
   cut up
½ cup (125 milliliters) all-purpose flour
3 tablespoons (45 ml) butter
1 cup (250 ml) chopped celery
2 medium onions, thinly sliced
1 teaspoon (5 ml) seasoned salt
1 teaspoon (5 ml) salt
dash pepper
1 bay leaf
4 cups (1 liter) water
4 cups (1 l) beef broth
2 cups (0.5 l) diced carrots
4 medium potatoes, peeled and diced
4 ounces (115 grams) sliced mushrooms,
   quickly and lightly cooked in a small
   amount of butter, oil, or fat
¼ cup (60 ml) all-purpose flour
⅓ cup (75 ml) water

Directions
1. Coat the rabbit pieces with ½ cup (125 ml) of flour. Shake excess flour off the pieces.
2. Melt the butter in a pan over medium heat. Brown the rabbit pieces in the pan on all sides.
3. Add the celery, onion, salt, pepper, bay leaf, water, and beef broth to the pan. Heat the stew to the boiling point. Reduce the heat to a simmer, cover the pan, and simmer the stew for 2 hours.
4. Add the carrots, potatoes, and mushrooms. Cook about 30 minutes longer or until the vegetables are tender.
5. Combine ¼ cup (60 ml) of flour and ⅓ cup (75 ml) of water. Shake or stir the mixture until it is well blended and smooth. Stir the flour mixture into the broth. Heat and stir the stew until it is thickened. Serve and enjoy.

Small Game Report

Now it is your turn to go to work. Choose one of the small-game animals listed in the chart on page 7 of this book. Using this book, your school or local library, and the internet, write a report about hunting this animal.

Research tips:

Look for additional books about small-game hunting in your library under the Dewey Decimal number 799.2.

Useful search terms for the internet include "small-game hunting," along with

the name of your state or province, "tracking small game," "rabbit hunting," "squirrel hunting," or the name of an other small-game animal that you have chosen.

Key questions to answer:

1. Where is the animal found?
2. How do you track this animal?
3. When can you hunt for the animal?
4. Is there a special license required for hunting this animal?
5. Why do people hunt this animal?
6. What types of equipment can be used for hunting this animal?

Take Aim Quiz

1 What are three things that small-game animals are hunted for?

2 What is a bag limit?

3 What is beagling?

4 What is the most-hunted animal in North America?

5 What are varmints?

6 What is poaching?

7 Name at least three of the weapons that are used to hunt small-game animals.

8 What is blaze orange, and why is it used?

Key Words

biology: the study of plants and animals and how they live and grow

conservation: the protection and careful use of forests, rivers, minerals, and other natural resources

crossbow: a bow with a device that helps pull back and release the string

dressed: having the internal organs of a hunted animal removed to preserve its meat

ecology: the study of how plants and animals live in relation to each other and to their environment

habitats: places where animals or plants live or grow

hide: the skin of an animal, sometimes used to make leather

pellets: small metal balls that are shot from guns

pelts: skins of animals with the hair or fur still on them

pest control: managing a species that harms crops, property, people, and other animals

poisonous: having a deadly substance that causes illness or death

scavengers: animals that feed on other dead animals

species: groups of individuals with common characteristics

trigger lock: a metal or plastic lock around the trigger to help keep the gun from firing

Index

Log on to www.av2books.com

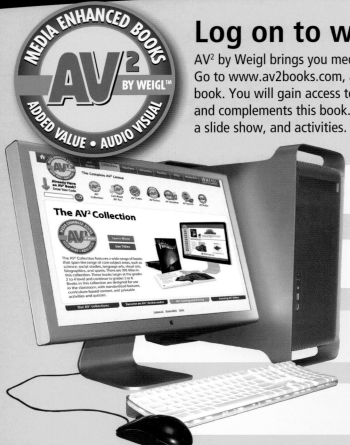

AV² by Weigl brings you media enhanced books that support active learning. Go to www.av2books.com, and enter the special code found on page 2 of this book. You will gain access to enriched and enhanced content that supplements and complements this book. Content includes video, audio, weblinks, quizzes, a slide show, and activities.

Audio
Listen to sections of the book read aloud.

Video
Watch informative video clips.

Embedded Weblinks
Gain additional information for research.

Try This!
Complete activities and hands-on experiments.

WHAT'S ONLINE?

Try This!	Embedded Weblinks	Video	EXTRA FEATURES
Complete a tracking activity.	Learn more about small game hunting.	Watch a video about small game hunting.	**Audio** Listen to sections of the book read aloud.
Identify small game animals.	Find the small game hunting rules for your state.	Watch a video about small game animals.	**Key Words** Study vocabulary, and complete a matching word activity.
Try this matching activity for small game hunting equipment.	Read more about hunting safety.		**Slide Show** View images and captions, and prepare a presentation.
Test your knowledge of small game hunting.			**Quizzes** Test your knowledge.

AV² was built to bridge the gap between print and digital. We encourage you to tell us what you like and what you want to see in the future.
Sign up to be an AV² Ambassador at www.av2books.com/ambassador.